THE PRACTICAL GUIDE
TO PROCESS SERVING

Second Edition

Wm. Stage, B.Ph.

Birkenfeld Press
St. Louis

Wm. Stage

The Practical Guide To Process Serving
Second Edition

Library of Congress Control No. 2001126226
ISBN 0-962-91242-5

Birkenfeld Press is an imprint
of Floppinfish Publishing Co. Ltd.
Post Office Box 4932
St. Louis, Missouri 63108
314.567.8697

FORWARD

✧ ✧ ✧

Do you enjoy driving far and wide, lost in subur-bia looking for some obscure street? Do you like to use maps? Do you like sleuthing? Working on your own schedule? Can you think on your feet and act quickly? Can you deal with adverse, sometimes hostile situations? Are you interested in the judicial system? Do you like to watch your bank account grow?

If you answered yes to these questions, then you may be cut out to be a special process server.

I became a special process server in the Spring of 1998. The original motive was to earn an additional $500 a month to help pay mounting bills. I wanted something flexible, something novel that would accommodate an already busy, sporadic schedule. I never wanted it to be full-time. I already had a job I liked, as a newspaper writer.

The year before, I had gone to court on a domestic matter involving my son. I recall sitting in a conference room at my lawyer's office, giving the names and addresses of five friends and associates to the process server who would serve the subpoenas so these people would testify on my behalf. As I wrote out the check for $150—thirty bucks per person—I wondered how one might go about becoming a process server. The server said that the St. Louis Sheriff's Department had a class which was held a few times a year and went for three evenings. Since taking that class, I have been enlisted to serve thousands of summonses, subpoenas and court orders, and have had no trouble in meeting my goal for extra income. In fact, after five years of doing this work, I made the switch from the primary occupation of journalist to that of process server. In short, I enjoy serving papers and it keeps the wolf away from the door.

The class was well-taught by two cadre of the St. Louis City Sheriff Department. To their credit, Maj. Greg Thomas and Lt. Ray Harris encouraged us as well as previous batches of plebes to call if we ever had problems in the field. They knew situations would arise that weren't covered in class. And indeed, those situations did arise. As I went about my business I began to see how things could be better accomplished by possessing a little more wisdom here, a little more patience there; by knowing when to tip your hand, as it were, and when to keep your hand close to the vest. While the Sheriff Department has a lesson plan for their process serving class, I could find no book on the subject, only sections in law textbooks. I thought to write a handbook that deals with the finer points of the job, speaks in plain language, and offers realistic situations that could be encountered. I have included personal anecdotes in places where I thought the point might be better elucidated. I hope this effort will be of practical use to the would-be process server, the novice process server or anyone interested in the arcane world of the process server.

Wm. Stage

St. Louis, Missouri
May, 2007

Let it be known: The following treatise is based on personal experience and the methods of service described herein may, as a matter of practice, be less or more involved. Service of process is articulated or defined by court rules and statutes and may vary from state to state. The practicing special process server should govern himself by the Rules of Civil Procedure pertaining to service of process in his home state.

"They of the Towne had servid process upon him."
— William Henry Turner, 1577
Selections from the Records
of the City of Oxford, England

"You've got to serve somebody."
— Bob Dylan, 1979

✍

WHO CAN BE A
SPECIAL PROCESS SERVER?

Although it is not widely known, court documents are routinely served by a unique contingent other than sheriff deputies. Known as special process servers or "specials," they are independent contractors hired to serve legal documents, or process, such as summonses, subpoenas, garnishments, and court orders. The preponderance of these papers involve cases that are civil in nature, [e.g. divorce and child custody, personal injury, breach of contract, etc.] as opposed to papers stemming from the criminal side. Service of process moves the judicial system along. Lack of service stalls the system.

The constitutional precept of due process requires that a defendant be given notice of legal action being taken against him. If the defendant has not received proper notice, the lawsuit is not engaged. Originally, the sheriff or, in some states, the constable, in whose jurisdiction the lawsuit pertains was the party to give notice, that is, serve process. It is still largely that way. However, as an alternative, most states permit the use of private process servers.

The qualifications for becoming a private or special process server are fairly broad: One must have attained a certain age, usually 18, and not be a party to the lawsuit—in essence, virtually any disinterested party. Other requirements may include showing proof of U.S. citizenship or undergoing a criminal record check that shows no felony convictions. Moreover, some places impose the additional requirement of licensing.

In order to serve process issued by the 22nd Judicial Circuit here in St. Louis, for example, one must take the sheriff's course in process serving and purchase what is called Errors and Omissions insurance. When the candidate has completed the three-evening course, at a $300 fee, and secured the insurance at around $550 per year [and going up], he or she is licensed for two years and will appear on "the list," a roster of approved special process servers eligible to be appointed by the circuit court judge.

A special may be hired either by a lawyer representing a client or by the client directly. A form, "Request for Appointment of a Special Process

Server," will be completed, and barring any problems, the special will be appointed by the court to serve process for that specific case. He will be appointed anew for each case he works on. Only the appointed individual is authorized to serve those papers; he may not pass them on to someone else to do the job.

True, there are judicial districts in which taking a class through the courts is not required, in which one need not be officially licensed to serve process. But there is an important distinction between the special process server who is out there serving papers without benefit of formal instruction and one who has taken the sheriff's course—one is armed with knowledge and one is not. Indeed, the rules and protocol of process serving are so varied and specific that the careless and/or ignorant process server could well botch the lawsuit. In fact, that's the reason for the insurance: protection in the event the hiring attorney or his client decides to sue the process server down the road for having ruined the case by serving the wrong person, filing a bogus return, or making one of any number of mistakes, deliberately or inadvertently.

In short, the question to ask yourself in deciding whether you really want to do this work is this: Am I prepared to take on serious responsibility?

WHY THEY CALL YOU

Attorneys don't call you because you're a swell guy or gal. They call you because the sheriff for whatever reason couldn't do the job, or because there's a time crunch, or because the situation requires special handling such as waiting for someone to appear or being in a certain place at a certain time.

The sheriff's office usually gets first crack at service and that is because the cost of serving the process is included in the filing fee. It is estimated that the sheriff's success rate is about 70 percent and what's left undone often goes to the special process server. In other words, specials tend to get the more difficult cases. Even so, if you are a diligent process server your success rate should be at least 75 percent. Because unlike the deputy process server for the district who has scores of papers to serve, your volume will be far less, perhaps fewer than a dozen. And you, being dogged in nature, are going to visit these locations again and again, at all hours, until you either achieve service or determine that the subject is unavailable for service.

Most law firms have at least two special process servers on call. They use specials because we, by reputation, are willing to go the extra mile to get the job done. This could mean staking out a location—a playground, a bar, a mall—waiting for a subject to arrive. It could entail having to be some place at 4 a.m. or driving great distances not even certain the subject will be available once you arrive. All these extras, of course, may be included in your charges.

As for the urgent job, that's what makes being a special process server so interesting. You may be picking lint from your navel at 2:30 on a Tuesday afternoon and the phone rings: Can you serve this summons by 5 p.m.? More often, however, you are engaged in some pursuit when that call comes, the call that wants you to drop whatever you are doing to accommodate that lawyer. Almost comically, they all think you work only for them. I cannot tell you how many times my somewhat planned-out day has changed, sometimes drastically, with the ring of a cell phone. All of a sudden I'm picking up four subpoenas and heading out to the Boonies.

Availability is key to the job. If you decline, that lawyer or legal secretary will simply go down the list and call around until he or she finds someone else to do it. And the next time that lawyer has a similar assignment they will likely call that person first. So, it behooves you to get to that lawyer's office, pick up the papers, and drive post-haste to the designated location. Again, you are the independent contractor and so you have the option to tack on an "urgent fee" or a "has-to-be-done-today" surcharge or whatever you choose to call it.

❧

WHAT YOU CAN
DO AND CANNOT DO

Your primary job is to serve papers for the lawyer and, by extension, the court. As such, you are an officer of the court. This is not the same as a sheriff's deputy or police officer. Some jurisdictions, such as the City of St. Louis, provide special process servers who have taken the class with an official photo-ID card. You may show this card all you want, and at times it will be necessary to get you past the gate, but you should never represent yourself as being a member of a law-enforcement organization. You are not authorized to carry a badge or to make an arrest. However, in certain situations in the work environment—say, a receptionist or security guard preventing or interfering with your attempt to serve an individual who is known to be on the premises—you may call the police and request assistance. More on this later.

Perhaps the special process server's greatest value is

the ability to cross jurisdictional lines, something which the sheriff's deputy or police officer may not do. Say you are appointed to serve a summons which originates in the 21st Judicial Circuit of the County of St. Louis, but, once you visit the address on the summons, you learn that the defendant in question has moved two counties over. You may go to that county and serve the papers. Say the defendant has moved to Puerto Rico. You may travel to Puerto Rico to serve that person, as long as the attorney is willing to foot the bill.

WEAPONS

Under Missouri law any person authorized to serve process may carry a concealed firearm, but a rule in the City of St. Louis modifies that carte blanche authorization with the stipulation the special may carry the weapon only while actually engaged in the service of process. Now, an active process server always has someone he's trying to find and therefore could honestly maintain, under questioning, that he was going to or coming from a job.

The weapons-status card for special process servers issued by the city of St. Louis has two categories: "armed" and "unarmed." To be listed as armed, the special must own the weapon and have qualified at an approved target range with that weapon. One local indoor target range used by process servers and private security guards offers firearms qualification. The four-hour session, including the price of ammunition, costs under $100.

The licensed special process server may also opt

not to carry a firearm. His or her weapons-status card will then be marked "unarmed." In my world, a cell phone and a canister of pepper mace is better than a handgun while out in the field serving papers. The pepper spray is more for dogs than people.

The handgun is really not called for simply because it's unlikely that someone will try to shoot you merely for knocking on his door. And if this person does decide to open fire what are the chances that you, the intrepid process server, will be able to get the drop on him? Instead, it's far more likely that this reprobate will become belligerent and decide to take a poke at you. In such a case, I would leave and call 911. Besides, it's hard to conceal a handgun in the summer when wearing only shorts and a T-shirt. Another precaution against assault is to take a course in self-defense.

﹏

WHAT YOU WILL NEED

Y ou don't need much to be a good process server. A dependable vehicle is essential. I find myself driving 75 to 150 miles a day on both city streets and country roads. On the job, your vehicle is your office. Therefore, you will need at the ready good maps and street guides for the territory in which you work, a flashlight, a camera, a cell phone, a phone book, and a notebook for notating attempts. You will also need a home computer or laptop with a link to the Internet.

You will become adept at finding the most obscure addresses imaginable. This will be accomplished by using various street guides. The commercially published street guide for any given county is okay, but even better is the utility-company street guide. It's more comprehensive, the streets are shown in greater detail, and the street names are in larger print. You can't buy these at the store; the only way to get one is to know somebody at the gas company or the electric company.

Sometimes you don't need the detail; you need the overview. What's the best way to get from this suburb to that suburb on the other side of the city? For that, you need a good overall map of the city, showing all the major arteries. The flashlight and magnifier are necessary because unless you have the eyesight of a barn owl you are going to have trouble reading the small print at night in the dimness of the average car-interior light.

The reason for the Internet hookup is MapQuest ®, a boon for anyone who travels afar seeking specific addresses. MapQuest® not only gives explicit directions but provides distance from base to destination, something you will find handy when making out your bill. You simply punch in an address and it tells you how to proceed; it may not be the most direct route but the directions will get you there. Some specials are using electronic GPS devices which can be mounted on a console or dashboard of the vehicle. Key in your next stop and this device will actually talk you through the turns, the one-way thoroughfares, the zigs and zags of the maze we call a city.

The camera is for documentation. If you work

serving papers the chances are excellent that you will be asked to photo-document any number of things such as places where accidents occurred, unsafe work conditions, post-collision vehicles in tow lots, people working despite doctor's orders, etcetera. Some of it is up-front and some of it is surreptitious. It's up to you what adjunct work you accept.

The forms you will need may be made on any personal computer. They consist of an affidavit of service [the return] for the court, and stationery with letterhead for reports and invoices. We'll discuss the uses of the forms later.

⌁

KEEP TO THE TRUNK OF
THE TREE: TYPES OF SERVICE

In the world of lawsuits there are two prime lessons to be learned: First, the system does not work unless the process gets served. Second, when the papers are served, they had better be served right. **Personal service** is the best and least disputed kind of service. If due process could be likened to a tree, personal service is the trunk of the tree. Personal service means that you have made contact with the person you believe is the person to be served. You are actually in his or her presence, that is, he or she is standing in front of you, or looking at you through a screen door or window or in some other manner that would allow you to identify that person in court if called upon to do so.

With this type of service, as with all types of personal service, you have identified yourself as a process server or officer of the court and you have told that person he or she is being served with legal documents. You don't need to give your name, nor do you need to explain yourself before you serve the individual. The moment of service is a good time to say, "I'm a process server, and I have this summons [or legal document] for you." The subject accepts it, and you walk away. The best outcome is when the defendant/respondent willingly accepts the process. When typing your return affidavit, you may note: personal service by hand delivery.

Another form of personal service is **service by touch**. In the event the defendant/respondent refuses to accept the document after the process server has identified himself and his purpose, the process server may touch the person with the document. After that, the papers are dropped to the ground at the feet of the defendant/respondent. The summons and carefully crafted petition may blow away or get run over by a bus, but he has been served nonetheless.

It has become obvious that some people believe if they don't physically take the papers they are not served. Or, if they don't sign for the papers they are not served. This assumption is incorrect. If I am certain that person in front of me is my man and he will not take the papers I am offering with outstretched arm, I will say something to the effect: "You can either take the papers or not take them. You're still served anyway." Then I brush the papers on his torso and drop them to the ground. In such an event, some people will heatedly dispute the action, stating, "I know the law and you haven't served me, blah, blah, blah." There is absolutely no sense in responding to this argument. As long as you are certain he is the individual to be served, you will leave the papers where they fell and inform him that he is served.

Service by touch can even become quite dramatic. I have had situations where I was actually racing to beat the defendant to his car, trying to tag him with papers before he could jump in the front seat, lock the door and drive off. There were times I missed by two seconds. However, touching his car with the papers as he peels out from the curb will probably not be considered good service in most courts. In fact, it could be said to be getting out onto the shaky branches of the tree.

Sometimes the defendant/respondent has an astute lawyer who decides to challenge service. In such instances, a judge will scrutinize the method of service detailed on the Affidavit of Service that the server has filed with the court. The special may be called to court to testify as to the circumstances of the service. Maybe it transpired that the defendant came to the door but would not accept the papers. The server was unable to touch this person with the process but then acted by reading to this person the salient parts of the summons or subpoena. **Reading to And within hearing of** the defendant is considered a form of personal service but watch out, for it can suddenly lead you out on to precarious branches. It only works if you have positively identified the individual in question and if you are certain they have heard the words spoken. Let's say at the start of your oration, the subject retreats into the house, shutting the door behind her. With the subject no longer visible, how can the server be certain she heard the full recitation? Hearing this, the judge would likely nullify the service and the process server would have egg on his face.

Once in a federal building I served, in a rather ridiculous manner, a subpoena to a woman as we both rushed down a hallway, she trying to get away and I trying to keep pace and read at the same time. As she ducked in to a restroom I finished reading in the hallway, using a voice so clarion that the entire floor of bureaucrats surely must have heard. I then dropped the subpoena to the floor and left. It would have been far less embarrassing for her had she taken the papers to begin with. In that case, as to method of service, I would put on my affidavit: Personal Service: reading to and within hearing of the defendant.

You must remember to leave a copy of the process at the location where you do the reading. If you do the reading at the front door to the home, leave it there, outside the door. Do not drop the document in the mail slot.

By accomplishing personal service you have not only notified the defendant of the proceedings against him or her but you have established evidence of their presence.

Due process doesn't require that the defendant be served personally. In Missouri, **copy service** or substitute service is accomplished by leaving the summons and petition with a spouse or member of the immediate family over 15 years of age, of sound mind, and who shares the same abode as the defendant/respondent. This type of service will only do when attempting to serve an individual, not a business or corporation. Copy service may be made only at the usual place of abode, generally the residence, of the party named in the lawsuit, and not at the place of employment, the supermarket, or the football game. That would not be good service.

Copy service does not work for the service of a subpoena which must be served only on the individual named on the document.

The process server need not make a serious attempt at personal service before going the route of copy service. It may be on the first attempt that the spouse, parent or offspring of the defendant answers the door. The process server must use his discretion as to whether the individual standing before him is a suitable candidate on whom to perform copy service. To do so the server must inquire as to the individual's relationship to the defendant. A suitable person for accepting the process does not mean, as some attorneys may try to tell you, the cleaning lady or the gardener. Many process servers consider the live-in paramour a legitimate person to accept service in lieu of the defendant. Again, this is getting away from the trunk of the tree and out on to a shaky branch. You don't know the true relationship of that person, standing at the door in her undies, to the defendant; she may have kicked him out of the house three weeks before and she hopes never to see him again.

Keep in mind that these alternative methods of service may well be scrutinized by the courts, and with copy service the rule of thumb generally applied when assessing validity of service is that the person copy-served should be so closely related to the defendant that there is a great likelihood that the defendant will receive notice in a timely manner.

This rule will be your guide more often than you might imagine, for in any metropolis there are legions of people who do not have one constant address. They crash at this place for a couple days, they "stay" at that place for a week or two. So often it happens that the address on the summons goes to the mother or the sister or some other relative of the defendant. You won't know that until you get there and are told, "Kerry doesn't live here. We don't know where he stays. He just comes around once in a while." You will quiz them as to the frequency of these visits. If you are told he drops by every Sunday for pot roast then there is a good chance that the process will get to him. On the other hand, if you leave the papers with Aunt Toad who tells you she hasn't seen her nephew, the defendant, for a month and doesn't plan on seeing him anytime soon then, essentially, you are violating that guy's civil right to due process. You will be stating on your return affidavit that he is served when, in fact, there was not a great likelihood he would receive notice of the legal action being taken against him. Let your sense of fairness be your guide.

One pitfall of copy service is the kid who looks 15 and who tells you he is 15, but is in fact 13. The respondent may well get the summons, but if his attorney wants to challenge service he could make a case.

You may encounter a situation where a valid member of the defendant's family, the spouse for example, refuses to accept the document, saying something like, "You'll have to come back when he's here." If, in fact, you have established that he or she is a legitimate person upon whom service may be achieved, then, despite this person's protest, she gets the summons. However, it is important that you somehow elicit her name because you need to include that name on your return of service affidavit. If you cannot learn her name you will have to put down a description of this person along with her relationship to the defendant, as was told to you. Example: "I'm his sister."

If all this sounds daunting, don't worry. The good news is that the preponderance of papers in your satchel will get served. Why? Because the human urge to accept something offered—even a sheaf of official-looking papers—is very powerful indeed.

FOREIGN PAPER

The term **foreign paper** describes legal documents that originate in jurisdictions outside the one in which service is to be made. Most often, they are out-of-state summonses. Papers must be served in accordance with the rules of the jurisdiction in which they were issued. They usually come with instructions, perhaps the Rules of Civil Procedure regarding service of process for that state, on what is acceptable service.

＊

THE SUMMONS

A summons is issued to notify a defendant that a legal action has been brought against him and that he is required to respond within a certain period under penalty of default. It also may serve to notify the defendant to appear in court to answer an action which has already been brought against him. This type of summons will have a court date and venue.

The summons itself is usually a one-page form that is generated by the circuit clerk's office. Attached to it will be a petition also called a complaint that has been drafted by an attorney or, in some cases, by the plaintiff/petitioner himself. When the process server files his return it should state that he served "a summons with petition," for example, or "a summons with motion to modify."

The summons is serious business. It either engages the respondent/defendant in a lawsuit or it affects the lawsuit in which he is already involved. The moment you serve this individual his life will change in some way, and it may well be for the worse. The long-term result may be a drain on the pocketbook, and at the very least this individual will consider hiring a lawyer. No wonder he may be trying to avoid you.

Kinds Of Summonses

Besides the regular summons, there are several other species such as the Juvenile Summons, the Probate Court Summons, and the Landlord Summons. We will look at them briefly, one by one:

Juvenile Summons may be attached to various Juvenile Court actions such as mistreatment, transfer of custody, adoption, or delinquency. The juvenile summons is generally served upon the parent or guardian of a minor. Often the parent or guardian is being ordered to appear before a judge or commission for a hearing on the matter and is further ordered to bring along the child in their custody. The special process server may be called upon to serve this type of summons. Sometimes, though, the serving officer may be commanded to take children into custody, place them in detention, or turn them over to some state agency. In that case, it will likely be the sheriff's deputy undertaking the service.

The **probate-court summons** may be attached to a

notice, a petition, order, warrant or any other type of probate process. Personal service is best, but copy service is acceptable. Certain probate petitions involve involuntary hospitalization or appointment of a guardian. If the special determines that the subject is mentally deficient or out of touch with reality, he should read the summons and petition in the presence of a family member and then leave the true copy behind. If the subject is hospitalized or resides in a nursing home, suggest that a nurse or staff administrator witness the service.

Some process servers make their living by working for property management companies, doing only **landlord summons**. This is a process used by landlords to secure unpaid back rent or to start the eviction process. This summons with petition is served to the tenant or tenants, setting a court date at which time both parties may present their evidence. Personal service is best; copy service is acceptable.

Often, landlord summonses are stamped **"serve or post."** This means that in lieu of personal service the summons may be posted on the front door or some patently visible place near the entrance to the dwelling. It is probably not a good idea to pound the document into the building with hammer and nail;

duct tape will do nicely.

Any time something is posted there is a mailing requirement. When the special process server does a posting he will file two returns with the court: A regular certificate of service stating that he posted the summons, and another notarized **affidavit of mailing** stating that, in addition to posting the summons and petition, he sent by regular mail and by certified mail another copy to the tenant. Essentially, this affidavit will state that on a given day, "I have mailed a copy of the summons and petition to the defendant's last known address by ordinary mail and by certified mail, return receipt requested." He will provide the certificate number of the letter mailed and a statement that the mailing was done at least ten days before the return date of the summons. If the certified letter does get signed, and that is not the norm, it will come back to the process server and he will include that proof in his return.

Landlord summonses fall into two categories: the regular summons and the **unlawful detainer**. Say, the rent is paid up but the tenants play their music too loud. The landlord gives them written notice of 30 days in which to move. They will not move. They are unlawfully detaining his property. The landlord goes to court and files an unlawful detainer action—as opposed to the landlord action. The process server will attempt to serve this summons personally on the tenant, although if it is not served by the court date the landlord may return to court and get an order of publications, which is a "post only" document and the regular mailing requirements apply.

In short, the landlord summons is the legal tool to secure unpaid rent. If the rent is paid, but the landlord wants the tenants to move anyway he seeks to oust them with an unlawful detainer. With a landlord summons, the landlord can get the serve or post which will usually hasten the judgement, presumably against the obstinate tenant. The unlawful detainer is generally a more drawn-out process, possibly putting the process server to work twice—attempting personal service and, if unsuccessful, posting and mailing— all toward one end, the removal of unwanted tenants.

Time Limitations on a Summons

All summonses have a finite period in which to be served. When you receive a summons, pay attention to the dates, specifically the date it was issued or else the court date. For some reason lawyers sometimes hold onto these papers after they receive them from the courts. Ideally, you should have two to three weeks to serve a summons and petition. Instead, you may be handed a summons that is close to the end date for valid service, or even past the date.

Summons from the Circuit Court generally have a time limit of 30 days from the date of the seal for the service to be made. If service is not accomplished by the end of 30 days the summons is no longer valid.

Summonses issued by Associate Circuit Court, sometimes called "money papers," have a court date. These are required to be served no later than 10 days in advance of that court date. If the court date is June 15, you would count backwards 10 days; the deadline for serving the paper would be midnight June 5.

Landlord Summons dealing with rent and possession of property must be served no later than four days prior to the stated court date or, if permitted, posted up to ten days prior to the stated court date.

Consequences of Ignoring A Summons

If the individual named on the summons knows she's been served in a civil suit and understands that she has been named as the defendant in that civil suit, yet fails to hire an attorney or otherwise answer the action, then a default judgment may be taken against her. As a consequence, her wages could be subject to garnishment and her property could be subject to execution [loss], or both. In that event, under Missouri law, she would have a year to try to set aside the default judgment. Her attorney would need to file a motion, stating the reason why the client didn't answer in a timely fashion in order to show the court that the failure to answer the lawsuit wasn't intentional or recklessly designed to impede the judicial process. In short, the attorney must show that the individual had some sort of valid defense and did not ignore the summons merely out of arrogance, conceit or the same sort of contempt for legal process that some people display when they tear up their parking tickets and throw them to the wind.

THE SUBPOENA

The subpoena is a whole different animal from the summons. The lawyer need not go to the circuit clerk to have a subpoena issued but generates the document at will from blank subpoenas kept in the office, as long as they are signed [signature stamped] by the circuit clerk. Also, the special process server does not have to be appointed to serve a subpoena. Most importantly, the subpoena must be served only to the individual to whom the subpoena is directed and it must be personal service. Otherwise stated, substitute service is not permitted.

There are two types of subpoena: The first is the ***subpoena ad testificandum*** commonly called a "regular subpoena." This subpoena commands an individual to appear and give testimony. It may be for the actual trial or, if leading up to the trial, the appearance may be scheduled in a law office, or some other place of the lawyer's choosing. This paper can be relatively easy to serve especially if the witness is not a party to the lawsuit and is friendly toward the suitor whose attorney issued the subpoena. An example: Melinda was involved in a rear-end collision. Her friend Rene was a passenger at the time of the accident. Rene wants to set the record straight as to what happened. She wants to testify for her friend. She will make a point of being at home when the process server arrives. Why then does Rene even need to be served? If she's such a good friend, won't she simply show up at the deposition without coercion? Probably, but human nature is so fickle that you never know what someone is going to do, and the attorney needs to know. He has arranged for opposing counsel to be present and hired a court reporter for the occasion. The subpoena is a formality. It commands the witness to appear. It is meant to impress on the witness that she is involved in a serious matter.

Often the witnesses to be subpoenaed are professional persons whose testimony is needed to bolster a lawyer's argument. These people will receive a witness fee, although it is often meager and nowhere near commensurate to what they would have earned had they not been ordered to sit in court, awaiting their turn on the stand. In attempting to serve subpoenas, the process server will be running after physicians, psychiatrists, social workers, architects, engineers and others with degrees after their names. Generally these people will not be happy about being served. Their time, they may feel, is too precious for court matters. Indeed, they are too important to deal directly with a process server. This attitude is conveyed, even instigated, by many receptionists who may put up a smoke screen for the boss. Expect to be kept waiting in reception areas, to be told the subject is at a hospital or out in the field and there is no way to know when she will return.

If you believe the witness to be served is on the premises, you can counter the uncooperative gatekeeper by reading aloud the state statute covering interference with the service of process. This has the effect of causing discomfort among patients or clients who happen to be present, especially when you get to the part where you say that failing or refusing to make the employee [the person to whom the subpoena is directed] available for service is a class C misdemeanor. That little announcement may just break the ice.

Police officers and detectives are routinely subpoenaed for testimony. They are served so often that the department has a system in place for accepting process. In the city of St. Louis, for example, the

Court Liason Office, a subsection of the circuit clerk's office, accepts subpoenas for cops and plainclothes officers on two conditions: The subpoena must relate to them as employees of the police department and not as private citizens, and the date of appearance is seven working days or more hence. Otherwise, the process server must locate the officer and deliver the subpoena by personal service.

Civil Procedure does not say that the subpoena may be accepted by someone else on behalf of the named witness. However, you will learn that there are a few exceptions, and only a few. Again, cops are one exception. Also at the municipal level, at least in St. Louis, the mayor and the Board of Police Commissioners have designated persons who accept subpoenas on their behalf, but only if they are being served in their capacity as civil servants. The service is duly noted in some ledger book and the subpoena, probably one of many for that week, is handed over to the city counselor's office. The special process server will learn these ropes over time.

Sometimes the special will get a slew of subpoenas to be served in the days before a particular case comes to trial. Five or six are not uncommon, and such a assignment can be easy especially if the subpoenas are directed to places of business and not to individuals who must be tracked down. These subpoenas must be served with alacrity and woe to the process server if the witnesses live far afield. Not long ago I was hired to serve subpoenas on three individuals who either lived or worked two counties away. There was a time crunch and I was having problems getting the final person, a surveyor. I made four attempts, each one a 120-mile round trip, and finally served him in his pajamas early one morning. In that case the mileage fee far exceeded the base fee for service, but it had to be done.

Sometimes it happens that some or all these witnesses will be targeted for subpoena by the "other side," that is, the opposing counsel. I have experienced situations where each witness I encountered and served would say something to the effect of, "I don't understand. I just got one of these yesterday." Indeed, another process server, my doppelganger, as it were, was also on the case, tracking the same witnesses and getting there before me. To make matters even more confusing for the witnesses, the two subpoenas they received instructed them to appear in court on different days. Such a situation could be intentional, the strategy of two separate lawyers, or it could be a miscommunication. Meanwhile, the witness needs to know whether he should take one day or two off work. Fortunately, it is not your problem.

Such confusion may often be cleared up by a phone call to the lawyer who issued the subpoena. In fact, at the bottom of the subpoena there is the notation "the date and hour that your testimony shall be required cannot be stated with certainty," and it goes on to instruct the witness to call the attorney on a certain day, usually the day before the scheduled testimony, to be "further instructed concerning your appearance." This notation is meant as a convenience to the witness, a way of anticipating the vicissitudes of a crowded and unpredictable docket, but the witness should be made to understand that unless otherwise instructed he is not excused from making an appearance at the time and date stated on the subpoena.

The second type of subpoena is the **subpoena duces tecum**, Latin for "bring with you." This process commands a witness to produce some document or record pertinent to the lawsuit and to bring it to the hearing or trial. The witness will often be someone at a business who has possession or control of the document in question. Rarely does this subpoena give a specific name of the witness to be served; rather it will address the "custodian of records" or "corporate designee."

There are two distinct types of situations here: The small business and the corporation. In the case of the small business, the server should go to the address provided on the subpoena, walk in and ask for the office manager. There is always an office manager somewhere. If you start out asking for the custodian of records you will likely get puzzled looks. That title probably doesn't exist in this office. Now, the office manager may refer you to the owner, the business manager, the bookkeeper or whomever. That's okay because then this person can accept service. However, if no one wants to accept service you will give the subpoena to the office manager or supervisor, somebody in charge, and you will get their name and title for the record. You will tell the individual politely yet firmly that she has been served and, if she has any questions, to call the lawyer whose phone number is shown on the subpoena.

The corporation is easier to serve. They probably get subpoenas routinely, and there will likely be a system in place for accepting process. Simply tell the person at the front desk that you have a subpoena for the corporate designee or whatever entity is named on the subpoena. The receptionist will call the correct person who will then come to the lobby. Or the receptionist may direct you to some cubicle and the job will be done forthwith. Again, you will get the name and title of the person who accepts service.

If the receptionist or some other company honcho tells you that the subpoena must be served at corporate headquarters which is in another state, you should counter by stating that when a company does business in a particular state it must accept service in that state.

Time Limitations on a Subpoena
Subpoenas for trial or a hearing may be served any time up to the date and time of the trial or hearing. Depending on the importance of the witness, certain lawyers will instruct the process server to serve the subpoena at all costs, even as late as the evening before the trial. However, the person who is served with such late notice can usually make a case that there is no time to prepare. They may contact a lawyer who will try to quash the subpoena. Nonetheless, you have done your job. Subpoenas for deposition generally must be served no later than seven days prior to the deposition.

Consequences For Ignoring A Subpoena

Some folks, you will find, don't take the service of a subpoena seriously. They will tell you they can't miss work or that they will be lazing in the Bahamas that day or offer the cavalier comment that they will "try to make it." The state commands the named witness "to lay aside all pretenses and excuses" and appear before a court or judge at a particular place and time.

What happens if that person does not show? The literal translation of the Latin word subpoena is "under punishment." If the witness chooses to defy the state's command, he is in contempt of court. The attorney who had him served can ask the judge to issue a **writ of attachment**. This writ [also known as a body attachment] authorizes the sheriff to find that person and physically haul him in to court. Some people have to learn the hard way.

In this event, the server's return will be scrutinized to ascertain that the individual was properly served under the rule of law. The server may even be suddenly summoned to court to testify that he did indeed serve the "failure-to-show" in person and to describe the circumstances and give a description of the witness. With any luck, for the sake of the server's reputation, this testimony will corroborate the information on the return, and the return should reflect exactly how the service was made.

~⌣~

THE COURT ORDER

The most common court order the process server will be called to serve is the adult abuse / stalking **ex parte order of protection**, also called a "restraining order." What this document means is that a person, the petitioner, has stood before a judge, without the offending party present, stating that she has been the victim of another who has threatened, physically struck, or stalked the petitioner—or some member of the petitioner's family who is perhaps too young, too old, or not mentally competent to come to court to make the complaint. Once served, the person named on the order, the respondent, will have an opportunity to stand before the judge [Missouri law states it shall be done within 15 days] and be allowed to tell his side of the story. There are, after all, two sides to every story. The judge, among other things, may agree with the respondent that the petitioner fabricated lies and acted out of vindictiveness and that the order of protection is rescinded. Or, the judge may agree with the petitioner and issue a full order of protection, generally good for 180 days.

Meanwhile, between the time the respondent is served and the time he appears before the judge to offer an explanation, he must comply with all the conditions of the order. This may mean, for example, that a man must not go near his children or wife or that a woman must suddenly pack her belongings and leave her home. It could mean that one employee cannot speak to or go near another employee, in or outside the workplace. This is nothing less than devastating for many people. The respondent, upon being served, often feels wounded, betrayed, infuriated, unglued, mortified, murderous and every other strong emotion known to man. Therefore, a very real element of risk and danger is involved, more so than in serving other types of paper. More police officers and deputies are injured in dealing with domestic violence than in any other assignment. In short, the special process server assigned to serve the ex parte order should never approach the job with a nonchalant attitude.

For this order the special process server may be hired by a private attorney representing the petitioner or by the petitioner directly. Usually, when the judge issues the order, it is passed on to the sheriff's department to be served. However, if the petitioner has talked with a lawyer and that lawyer believes the matter would be better handled through the efforts of a special, the lawyer will complete a request for appointment of special process server and the special will be notified as to when and where to pick up the service copy of the order.

If the sheriff gets first crack and has not been successful by the deadline then the petitioner, if still intent on lawful protection, must return to court to have a new order issued. It is then, on the second try, that the special is likely to be summoned. The petitioner will be handed the list of approved process servers for that jurisdiction and told to give one of them a call. The petitioner doesn't know one special from another. She may ask someone in the room to recommend somebody. If you want this kind of work, think about giving a pile of business cards to the clerk in the division that handles orders of protection.

Attempting to serve these ex parte orders has become almost a specialty for me. I get calls from people, usually women, who have come to the Adult Abuse office in the County Courts complex: The sheriff couldn't serve this guy. Will you be my process server? When I meet with these people, in a restaurant or gas-station parking lot, to pick up the service copy of the order and payment, I am sometimes amazed to learn the relationship between petitioner and respondent. Sisters petition for protection from their brothers, mothers ask for protection from their sons, daughters from their mothers. Hale young men petition for protection from their in-laws. It's like a soap opera and you, the process server, are the messenger among the actors.

More often, however, in my experience, the orders are taken out against non-family, specifically guys who can't seem to take no for an answer. What began as flirtation has become aggression; spurned advances have resulted in vindictive behavior—nasty phone calls at home or work, poison pen letters, threatening notes left on the windshield. Any of these actions will be checked off on the order under the heading "stalking."

During that initial brief meeting between petitioner and the server, the petitioner sometimes wishes to explain the story leading up to his or her visit to the judge. When this occurs, I am reminded of Edward Woodward's character in the 1980s television series *The Equalizer*. Woodward played a retired CIA operant or some sort of ex-lawman who had a standing ad in the paper offering to help people in trouble when all other avenues had failed. He was really good at his work, turning tables on the reprobates who bullied and preyed on the folks who came to him, the lambs of the world. And because the Equalizer was independently wealthy, he only helped the people he felt were worthy of his help.

That's where the comparison ends. I meet with the petitioner, listen to her tale of woe [being careful not to offer any advice, legal or otherwise], get the service copy of the order, a description of the respondent and hopefully a summary of his movements and hangouts. But, unlike the Equalizer, I do not have the luxury of turning away business because someone came on bumptious or smarmy. And, most important, I get payment up front.

Having accepted the job, the special should respond as quickly as possible. The petitioner is waiting anxiously for word that the respondent has been served. She wants that buffer of 200 feet, or whatever it may be, around her and which the *persona non grata* may not transgress. She already has a copy of the order, given to her by the court. This copy is to show to the police if a violation of the order takes place. However, the order is not in effect until the process server obtains service on the respondent. In Missouri, copy service is acceptable service for the ex parte order of protection.

It may be alleged that a child or minor who is under the supervision of the respondent is in danger from the respondent. The judge may grant the petitioner an **ex parte child order of protection**. Ex parte child orders of protection take precedence over all other process.

The special should read the complaint, usually penned in the petitioner's own hand, to learn what sort of person he will be dealing with.

Usually the special will find the respondent at home or work and hopefully he will not be in the presence of the petitioner. If all goes well, the respondent accepts the order without acting crazy or uttering something malicious-sounding. Great, you have served that person and, except for filing the return, your job is done. But if you are dealing with a marriage or live-in situation, things can get hairy. If both petitioner and respondent are present, the parties should be separated; you should then proceed to explain the action to the respondent. Obviously this may take some diplomacy, motioning a guy off to the side to tell him he has five minutes to pack his bags and get out of his own house. He may comply without problem; he may not. If the order calls for the respondent to leave the premises and he does not do so, the police should be called. If an assault occurs, the police should be called. This reinforces my previous assertion that a cell phone is a more valuable tool than a handgun.

The special should make a return posthaste so immediate proof exists that the order has been served. If the respondent, on being served, makes any threatening remarks directed at the petitioner such as, "You think this paper is going to keep me from getting to that girl?" you should convey that to the appropriate party—the petitioner's attorney or the police.

Time Limitations on an Order of Protection
In Missouri, an ex parte adult abuse order of protection may be served up to no later than three days before the court date.

Consequences for Violating an Order of Protection
Under Missouri statutes the violator may be punished by confinement in jail for as long as five years and by a fine of as much as $5,000. Other states have similar

consequences.

Another order that special process servers routinely get is the **Order to Show Cause**. This order always stems from the area of domestic law. It is issued when facts are brought before the judge that one of the parties in a divorce, say, is not keeping to the terms of the court-ordered divorce agreement. Usually the non-custodial parent has failed to make his child support obligations or failed to pay his share of the medical expenses for his child. The order to show cause is essentially a summons and will always have a court date; the individual is being summoned to appear before a judge and offer explanation, if any, why he has failed to meet the conditions of the divorce agreement. Service on this order must be personal since failure to show for the court date may result in a warrant for the arrest of the individual.

‹◦›

GATHERING INTELLIGENCE

When you go to the attorney's office to pick up the summons it behooves you to study the paper as you will likely have questions that can be answered there on the spot. First, double-check the address. Is it the same on the summons as the petition? If the addresses are different, find out why. Often the addresses have been taken from drivers' licenses and other records that are years old. Over time, these addresses may have been transcribed by, say, two police clerks and three legal secretaries. The point is, clerical errors do occur, and it's better to spot them in the lawyer's office than waste time out in the field searching for bogus addresses.

Bad addresses are the bane of the process server, sending us off on all sorts of wild goose chases. Here's an example: I had a summons to serve but once I arrived at the apartment complex I was befuddled; there was one too many numbers on the address. Finally I realized that the extra digit was the apartment number; it was tacked on the end of the address with no indication that it was the apartment designator. It took time to figure that out, but it would have only taken a second for the secretary to type "Apt. 4" instead of putting the number 4 at the end of the address and assuming the process server would somehow divine what this meant.

Too often it turns out that the street name was misspelled or the street numbers were transposed. When it comes to transmitting data, people are sloppy. You shouldn't have to pay for their sloppiness with your time and gas. Along with many other process servers, I charge for bad addresses, usually 10 to 15 dollars extra, but only if I am actually put out, having driven a long way or spent considerable time verifying that the address is bad.

Next, ask the lawyer where the person to be served works. Simply put, when the subject is at work, he is trapped. You cannot make this person open the door of their residence and accept the summons, but there are laws compelling the receptionist or security guard at a place of employment to make their employee available to the process server. The St. Louis Sheriff's Department hands out laminated wallet-sized copies of these two germane statutes so that the process server can cite them to anyone trying to thwart a legitimate attempt to achieve service. If the "gatekeeper" still doesn't comply, the next step is to call the police.

In my experience, the police may or may not choose to get involved. Some are reluctant unless the matter is a criminal one. You may have to show the officer the law and convince him or her that the gatekeeper is committing a misdemeanor by interfering with you or refusing to make the subject available for service. I recently had to serve a summons on an employee of a spa. The first attempt I was told she was in a room giving a treatment and couldn't be disturbed. She would be on break in two hours, could I come back then? Although it was inconvenient for me I agreed, but when I returned at the designated time I was told she had left for the day. Was I being played? I was told she would be back at 9:30 the following morning. When I returned to the spa at that time, I was told she had clients scheduled all day and would not be available at all. It was clear they were covering for her. At that point I phoned 911 and explained the situation. Within five minutes an officer showed, spoke to the spa's owner, and an agreement was struck. The subject would be done with her treatment in 35 minutes. The officer and I would return at that time and, along with the subject, we would all go to a room where she would accept service. Calling the police for help in serving process doesn't always work; this time it worked beautifully.

Third, get a description of the person, a photo if possible. This is important because the person you will have confronted on the front porch of his home can deny his own identity and, without a good description, the process server really has no choice but to give the benefit of the doubt, to walk away, the paper unserved. I have had guys say to me, "Oh, that's my brother you're looking for." Or, "He's my cousin and he just comes and goes." But with a decent description, perhaps the valuable information that the defendant you seek has a lazy eye and a gold tooth, and the guy you're sizing up shows the same features, then you hand the summons to him, saying, "I have a description of George Marmaduke, and I believe you are him. You're served." He may protest; he may throw the papers at you. You must walk away. You should enter the incident along with description of the problematic individual in your notebook, so that if the service is ever challenged you will be backed up by your notes. By doing the initial prep work, there is less room for error on the street. Error leads to no service or bad service, and neither is what the client needs.

As mentioned earlier, often the special process server will get papers the sheriff has already attempted to serve. Look at the summons. If it reads "Alias," service has been attempted once before. If it reads "Pluries," service has been attempted two or more times. Try to ascertain why the previous attempts failed.

~∾~

THE RETURN

When you go to the law office to pick up the summons or subpoena, there should be at least two copies: one to serve and one to file with the court. Each copy will have a space marked "sheriff's return," usually on the reverse of the document and sometimes on the front. This obviously is for the sheriff's deputy to fill out, although the special process server may fill it out if he so chooses. He will put down the particulars asked for, and he will sign his name in the space normally reserved for the serving deputy. You may want to purchase a stamp which bears your name, title and special process server number for the judicial circuit in which you work.

While filling out the sheriff's return is optional for the special process server, the document that will accompany his every return on a summons, subpoena and what-have-you is the **affidavit of service**. This is your personal statement of truth in the matter of the document you have been hired to serve. Once filed with the court, it will become a matter of record. Lawsuits can turn on the veracity of the process server's return, and he or she is liable for any false statements made.

The notary public who notarizes the affidavit is not affirming that the process server performed the service he claims, only that the server signed a statement in the presence of the notary in which he claims to have performed the service. By signing the notarized return, he is swearing under oath that he performed the service as stated.

There is no one correct format in which to create an affidavit of service. However, all forms have certain common elements: the name of the process server, the date and time of service, the species of paper [summons, subpoena, order to show cause, etc.], case/cause number which may be found on the face of the document [example FC07-76549], the names of plaintiff and defendant [Cooper vs. Hooper], the name of person served, the address where this person was served, the means of service [personal, copy, on behalf of, etc.], the county and state in which service was made, and a space for the signature of the process server, along with an identification tag [e.g. Special Process Server No. 197, 22nd Judicial Circuit, City of

St. Louis]. A space for the notary public's stamp and signature is located near the bottom of the form. It is not a complex form; it can be created on a personal computer in a half-hour. To see examples of returns go to the circuit clerk's office in any courthouse and look in the basket marked "Specials" or "Incoming Sheriff's Return's."

Types of Returns

Process servers don't like to file **non est returns**, for, unless the subject has died or moved far away, this return is an admission of failure. The wording of this document—Affidavit: Proof of Service On A Non-Est Return—reads something like this: "Comes now John J. McGillicuddy, Special Process Server, and hereby states that with due diligence I attempted but failed to serve the attached:" Next the special states the case/cause number, the person on whom service was attempted, the primary location where the service was attempted, the reason for the non-est return, the name and ID tag of the person filing the return and a place for the notary's stamp and signature.

When you indicate the reason for the non-est return, be succinct. "Unable to locate at address provided" or "Subject is on vacation for three weeks and will return on May 5, 2007" is sufficiently explanatory. I recently filed a non est return stating, "Address given was that of female friend who says she sees respondent only on occasion and refused to accept summons. All other attempts to locate were futile." This explanation is almost too long, but I believed it was important to indicate that the address provided for the respondent was that of person whose relationship to the respondent was unclear and that I therefore chose not to use copy service via the questionable girlfriend.

Some specials do not file their returns themselves. They give the notarized affidavit to the attorney who hired them, and trust that attorney to file it with the court. I choose to file my own returns, for a couple of good reasons: First, I know that it got done; second, the courthouse is the place to meet lawyers who may just be in need of a process server. It never hurts to have business cards at the ready.

When the return is notarized, I make two copies and take them to the court. I stamp all three copies with the time-clock device that sits on the counter in the circuit clerk's office and put the original where it needs to go. Of the remaining two photocopies, I give one to the attorney along with an invoice; the other I keep for my records.

The return affidavit must be filed in timely fashion. In some cases, you will have ample time, and in others you will have served the process close to the expiration date. Those specials who file their own returns may wait until they have several to file at once instead of making numerous trips to the courthouse; however, the responsible special does not hold returns more than a few days and certainly not wait until the court date is nigh. What good is your return if it is called into evidence in a court of law and it is nowhere to be found?

ॐ

DOCUMENTATION

Right at the onset some jobs turn into what might be considered full-blown investigations into the whereabouts of the defendant/respondent. Maybe you were given an old address, maybe the fellow moves often. Perhaps in attempting to locate him you were directed from one place to another. You spoke to friends, neighbors, family members and associates of this person being sought; you tried to find him through the post office or some professional organization; you even conducted surveillance outside his suspected residence—and still you never found him. All such activity should be recorded in a log, which can be your notebook or a worksheet for that express purpose.

Every stop you make should be notated. Nothing complicated, simply jot down the address visited, time and date, name of subject attempted, along with what transpired [e.g. "no response" or "resident says subject moved out five months ago"]. If you made service then include the germane details such as name and description of the person served [e.g. Mike Marshall, brother of defendant, 40 to 44 years of age, approximately 6-foot-1, 220 pounds, short brown hair, brown eyes, glasses, handlebar moustache]. If service is ever disputed, you could be called in to court to testify on the matter, and this could be a year after the fact. Will you remember everyone you encountered? The entries made in your log are your back-up.

You will store these notebooks or logs in a place where they will be safe from the elements. Paper has a way of being ruined by mold and mildew.

⊸

THE NEGATIVITY FACTOR

Serving papers need not be a perilous job. In fact, often times it feels like being a courier, a glorified courier but a courier nonetheless. Yet, the perpetual question asked of me is: Do the people you're serving ever try to harm you? I answer that I get yelled at all the time by irate people. I get told to leave. I am the brunt of all manner of insults and barbs, particularly, "Get a real job." But only once in nine years have I had to call 911 because I felt threatened, and that involved the rather comical situation of a baseball bat-wielding woman who had me cornered on her porch.

The most likely situation in which a special might encounter physical resistance is when someone, a defendant for example, adamantly does not want to accept service and yet service must be rendered. There is a direct conflict of agendas and the process server is given no choice but to force the paper on the subject. By "force" I mean leaving the process with the individual while letting him or her know in no uncertain terms that he is served. When this happens the defendant feels disrespected and angry. Never mind that you, the special process server, are an officer of the court and any act of aggression directed towards you is a serious offense; if he is belligerent by nature, he will likely lash out. In that event, you will act accordingly—by walking away, by dialing 911, by using pepper spray, by any means that will remove you from the immediate situation with the least chance of bodily harm to either of you.

And while this is not a job for the timid, there are all sorts of ways to avoid situations which might lead to violence, most of them a matter of using common sense. For instance, do not enter someone's abode uninvited; do not engage in name-calling with your subject; and don't stick around after you've served someone.

IT'S ALL IN HOW
YOU FINESSE THE SERVICE

The first five to ten seconds after someone answers the door are critical, for it is in that time that you will usually know whether you can serve the papers to that individual at that address. Don't have the papers in your hand; this causes suspicion: "Legal-looking papers? Hmm, that can't be good." When I first started out I would have the subpoena or summons rolled up in an inside coat pocket or front pants pocket with a shirt or jacket over it so that it was obscured but when the time came I could whip it out, so to speak. Even better, I have found, is to tuck the papers inside the spiral-bound notebook that I carry to log my visits. Toting a notebook and a pen, you look official. You could be a housing inspector from the city, a social worker, a courier. The idea is to allay suspicion so that they feel comfortable opening the door.

Theoretically, the person answering the door doesn't

know who you are or why you're there. You could be a salesman, a neighbor or, like I said, a housing inspector. She simply has no idea. She's heard about desperados strong-arming their way in to decent folks' homes; she may talk to you through the window or through the closed door. Obviously, the most likely questions directed at you, the process server, will be Who are you? and What do you want? Say, for example, you are trying to serve a DeWayne Nichols at this address. You might take the forthright approach and reply, "Process Server. I have a summons and petition for DeWayne Nichols." She might then open the door but more likely she will remain on the other side of the door and keep pumping you for information regarding the nature of this summons. This is no good because you are giving her all your information and getting back very little from her. I have to believe the serving deputies from the sheriff department have little choice but to employ such a forthright approach, limiting their chances with perhaps an official-sounding declaration to the wary householder. But we specials can take certain liberties—not with the law but with the words we choose to communicate.

Thus, I have found that the phrase which works best, at least better than coming right out and blurting your actual mission, is to say, "I have a delivery for DeWayne Nichols." This is not a lie and in presenting yourself this way, as a delivery person, you have done two things to put her at ease: You have mentioned the name of someone in her family and you have indicated that you have something for that person, possibly something good. Often this small ruse gets the person to open the door and once that happens there is a good chance you may be able to accomplish service.

Okay, now this woman has opened the door. You can see her plainly and you can talk to her in a normal manner. Obviously, she is not DeWayne but you want to know if he lives there and if so what is her relationship to him. The exchange may go like this:

Woman: "Yes?"

Process Server: "Is DeWayne home?"

Woman: "No."

Server: "Oh, when will he be back?"

Woman: "Later on. Who are you?"

Server: "I'm a process server. I've got some papers for him."

Woman: "What kind of papers?"

Server: "Well, [hesitant] are you related to DeWayne?"

Woman: "I'm his mother."

Server: "It's a summons with a petition, and if you

and DeWayne both live here then you can accept these papers for your son."

Because you have already established that the subject lives there and in fact will be home later, the copy service is valid. Next you need the woman's full name. The affidavit attesting to copy service requires a description of the family member served to include gender, race, age, height, weight [or build], and other distinguishing features such as tattoos, eyeglasses, facial hair. Since I am lousy at guessing people's ages, I inquire while I have them standing before me.

Most lawyers will be happy with copy service as long as it is valid. However, you may determine that you have time on the document to serve DeWayne personally. You decide to return when he is at the residence. You know if that doesn't happen, you can still likely accomplish copy service on the mother. In that event, the exchange, after the woman states that she is Dewayne's mother, may go like this:

Server: "I'm sorry but I'd prefer to hand these papers to DeWayne directly. Can you tell me when he'll be in?"

Woman: "He gets off work at five, so he's usually here by quarter-to-six."

Now, you're getting somewhere. The next obvious question is "Oh, where does he work?" The mother, naturally cautious, will either tell you the truth, tell you a made-up place of employment, or explain that she would rather you not go to her son's workplace. Meanwhile, you have assessed her sincerity, and, judging by her demeanor and tone of voice, decided that she is telling the truth about DeWayne's returning home around 6 p.m. Now, DeWayne, on being told that a process server came around asking for him, may disregard you entirely when you next show up. But that is a chance you'll have to take. Truth to say, most specials will serve the papers when the first opportunity presents itself.

Here are a few suggestions you may find helpful:

When you drive up to the address in question, have the papers ready and within reach; the person you seek may be in the yard, coming from or going to his or her car, or generally accessible for only a brief period. Any delay may thwart success.

If an early morning visit is called for, wait until sometime after sunrise. People aren't apt to open the door at such an early hour, suspecting robbery or some sort of chicanery. Also, when knocking on someone's door, stand back so they can see you. You're a stranger. They are reluctant to open the door when you are standing right there.

Knock long. Sometimes people are predisposed at the time you show up and it takes them a while to get to the door. Also, try the back door, the side door. If there is no response, try the neighbor's door. The neighbors may provide valuable information even if it is to tell you that they never heard of your guy. You've driven a ways to get to your destination, you want to at least come away with something you can use to advance the case.

THE ELUSIVE SUBJECT
AND DUE DILIGENCE

The probability level of accomplishing service on the batch of papers in your satchel may break down to something like this: About 25 percent achieved on the first or second try; about 40 percent are achieved after three to five visits; another 15 percent achieved with five visits or more and the remainder are *non est*, that is, not served.

The scrupulous process server will give the job due diligence, which is considered to be at least three attempts at different times of day.

I firmly believe that on the initial attempt one's chances of getting service are equally probable at whatever time of day you choose to try. This is assuming you know nothing about the defendant, whether he works by day, by night or not at all, whether he lives alone or with others, etcetera.

You should make the first attempt as soon as possible. That way, you will know how to get to the location, what sort of neighborhood it is in, who lives at the residence and all sorts of helpful information.

Let's go through some likely scenarios:

The subject is away, and the person who answers the door: [1] says the subject doesn't live there and he's never heard of him; [2] says the subject moved away but that he doesn't know where; [3] says the subject moved away, then gives you the address; [4] says the subject lives there but doesn't know when he will return; [5] says the subject is at work, but won't reveal where that is; [6] says the subject died six months ago.

All of these responses mean only two things to the savvy process server: You need to come back at another time or you need to research the veracity of what you've been told. The subject's new address, and report of his death are possibly verifiable with some phone calls and legwork. Employment, sorry, there is no easy way to locate one's place of employment. The other responses—moved away but don't know where; never lived there—could be the truth but you can't just accept the explanation as fact and chalk the service up as a *non est*, saying, "Oh well, I tried." That address wasn't just picked randomly out of the phone book; the individual you seek has some connection to that address and you must figure it out: Does he live there or not?

Through all this inductive thought process, do not discount the intangible quality that is your own judge of character. Does this person providing the information that could set you on another search path seem to be telling the truth? A well-honed intuitive sense that sorts out truth-tellers from false witnesses will keep you from spinning your wheels.

Also, if you suspect at all that the person feeding you this information could be the sought-after subject and is in fact lying through his teeth, you should ask to see some ID. Of course the individual is not obligated to produce identification, but if they do then at least that possibility is ruled out.

Another possibility is that the home or apartment you seek does exist but is empty, derelict or boarded up or has been razed by demolition, fire or some other means. In this event you may go to the post office serving that ZIP code and put in a **Request for Change of Address or Boxholder Information Needed for Service of Legal Process** form with the manager of that station. A response may be immediate, or it may take a week. Obviously, you should also do this to ascertain information on the subject who is said to have moved out. I find that soliciting the post office yields usable information about ten percent of the time; many of the people you seek will be transient and don't care whether or not their mail is forwarded.

Meanwhile, you could go back to square one and request more information. You might ask the lawyer to talk to his client or request that you be given the client's phone number. Sometimes the client knows the defendant and, on being pressed, may provide additional information that was not given to the attorney during intake. The attorney may subscribe to certain helpful data bases such as Regional Justice Information System [REJIS]. Accessing such a database may yield a current address or even a former address which could be still be occupied by family members who could lead you to your subject. Also, Missouri and, likely, other states have arrangements by which a process server, utilizing a pre-assigned security access code, can phone the Department of Revenue in an attempt to obtain the address connected to the subject's drivers license. To get this privileged information the process server should be able to provide some combination of subject's full name with middle initial, date of birth, and social security number. Keep in mind there is no guarantee that even this information will be current.

You might also try the election commission in the city where your sought-after subject lives. Believe it or not, a voter's address is public record. They must give it to you upon request.

I estimate that one in six of the papers I receive turns in to an investigation, that is, the initial address is bad or the person sought no longer lives there. It is my feeling that the 40 dollar fee I charge includes a certain amount of research toward the goal of locating that individual. I will talk to neighbors, make phone calls, submit the request for change of address form to the postmaster. I will decide when I have done enough and at which point I should start charging by the hour—in addition to the base fee. When I get to that point, where the routine checks are exhausted and the next step involves arduous work, I will call the hiring attorney and explain the situation. He or she may not want to incur any additional costs.

ELECTRONIC SHIELD

Cell phones pose a new set of problems for the process server. I have had several instances where the subject to be served had no permanent address and no place of employment yet had a communication line open by way of a cell phone. Yes, sometimes they happen to be drug dealers. Generally, I could talk to these folks any time I called, but physically get to them? Only if they so wished. These devices have the unfortunate effect of giving their users the advantage over the situation. When called, the subject will interrogate you, the process server: "Yeah, this Darnell, What you want?" What will you say? "I've just always wanted to meet you"? No, only the truth will prompt these people to show up, and that's a big maybe. No ruse is convincing enough. You have little choice but to state the nature of your business: "I'm a process server and I've got some papers for you."

What kind of papers, they will press. Here it gets dicey. How specific are you prepared to be? If you explain that you have a restraining order to serve on him, courtesy of an ex-girlfriend, that will be the end of that conversation; he'll never agree to meet you. On the other hand, I've found that some guys are actually eager to get their divorce papers, and will gladly meet you to accept service. It's kind of a crapshoot, so perhaps the best thing to do is tantalize your subject with a little information and hope he will be curious enough to meet with you to find out what the issue concerns. You might say something to the effect of, "Well, I haven't read the particulars and right now it's out in my car."

You might add that you can't really divulge any information beyond that because you have no way of knowing that the person with whom you're speaking really is Darnell Dickens or someone pretending to be him. This matter is confidential, you might say, and you wouldn't want to breach that confidentiality.

After that, he will either agree to meet you or tell you to take a long walk off a short pier. If he agrees to meet with you, he will either be there or he will stand you up. Whatever the outcome, at least you tried.

⌘

ON BEING DECEITFUL, DUPLICITOUS AND DOWNRIGHT SNEAKY

One attorney had me sign an oath or declaration that, while under his employ, I would not do anything unethical which included misrepresenting myself to somebody I was trying to serve. At the time, I joked that this was like asking a snake not to be stealthy. This arena of what we might call clandestine operations is a very personal thing. Some days, it seems that everyone out there is trying to dodge you or dupe you. We need an edge on these folks, and if a disguise or a bogus phone call will help get the job done, then, we might say, why not?

We've all heard of the special process server who posed as a pizza delivery guy in order to gain access to a known evader. That's part of urban legend; the subject thinks he's getting a nice savory pizza when instead he's handed the culinary equivalent of moldy bread, a summons and petition. A process server I know was frustrated over a situation involving, again, an evader. The guy would come home at a certain time, and once in the driveway, would click open the garage door, drive in, close the door and go into the house from the garage. My colleague's solution was imaginative: He placed a stick in the driveway. When the subject came home, he chose to get out of the car to move the stick. It was then that the wily process server dashed from his car, parked curbside, to make his delivery.

There are other stories of sneaky—some would say resourceful—process servers hiding in trees, posing as a wedding guest and serving the father of the bride in the reception line, and even serving folks as they sat primly in church pews on Sunday morning. Be aware that this *modus operandi* can backfire on you. Some attorneys may not like it, believing that such monkeyshines reflect badly on them. They don't want to be associated with a server who would violate what they may consider the sanctity of a church. It can be a fine line to walk, but try to insure that your efforts are in line with the values and ethics of the attorney who hired you. On the other hand if the attorney blurts, "We need to get this knucklehead no matter what," then you know you have *carte blanche* to use any legitimate trick in the book.

You would not want to employ subterfuge, however, until you first encountered some degree of uncooperativeness. A friend once gave me an official cap worn by meter readers of the local gas company. I thought I would try it out on a first attempt in a rather dicey neighborhood. I assumed there would be a problem. I assumed wrong. When the respondent came to the door and willingly took the summons, her words were, "You didn't have to wear no gas company cap—I would've taken the papers." Later, the hiring attorney asked me if I had worn the cap in question. I admitted such and she said it was no big deal, only that she had heard about it. And though she acted like she didn't care about my attempt at disguise, even chuckled at the thought, she never called me again.

Still, there are things you can do that are only a little sneaky, and likely would not pose an ethical dilemma for the average process server. These things involve gathering intelligence on your subject; the more you know about the person the easier the job becomes. Here are some preliminary steps you can take; think of this as homework. If you have only a residential address look in the phone book to see if the person is listed. If so, call that number and ask for your subject by first name, say, Fred. The family member who answers may assume that you are a friend and tell you everything you need to know about Fred: Where he works, what time he'll be home, or the name of the bowling lanes where he goes for league night. If they act suspicious asking who you are and the nature of your business, politely say you'll try back later when Fred is home.

If Fred himself answers you will have to come up with something—wrong Fred, wrong number. Something.

Let's say the summons tells you to serve the individual at his place of employment. You could call ahead to see if that person is in the office or on the grounds all the time, or hardly ever. If he's a salesman or contractor he may check in only at the beginning of the day or the end of it. Some helpful receptionist may tell you precisely when you need to be there to talk to him in person.

I would make these phone calls to streamline my efforts and use my time more efficiently. If the address is nearby, on my flight-path as it were, I would simply go there and check it out. However, if it were 20 miles cross-town I would certainly rather make the trip when I had good information that the person would likely be there. You can dial a telephone company code [*67 in Missouri] if you don't want your name and phone number collected by Caller ID.

Caller ID can be a very helpful tool. Let's say you are trying to serve Rico, who has no known address. All that you have for him is a beeper number. You beep him and he calls back; with any luck he calls from a residence, leaving a name and phone number on the Caller ID. You can then call AT&T [or whomever] directory assistance [1411] and for a dollar get the address that is cross-referenced to that phone number. Ask for reverse locating. Now, with any luck, you've got something to go on, a physical address.

Also, there will be opportunities to snoop. Case in point: I once had to hike through the woods and up a small mountain to get to a secluded cabin, probably a weekend getaway for the defendant. There was no one home and no one around so I began peering in through the windows. Finally, after seeing his name and title on some correspondence and magazines that were discernible, I was able to conclude that this person was a realtor working in the St. Louis area. The next day I called the St. Louis Realtors Association and, sure enough, I was able to locate this person. As it turned out, he owned a real-estate company, and serving him was not a problem. Yet, the address I was given by the lawyer was 55 miles away, in another county. Without snooping, I probably would have made two more attempts, caught chiggers again, and wasted time and gas.

If all this sounds like so much Sam Spade stuff, remember that part of your job is to be nosy—okay, investigative, if you prefer. Employing small, harmless ruses, gathering intelligence surreptitiously and doing what you can do within the law will improve your success rate. You won't be known as the process server who is fourth down the law firm's list to call, the one who files every third return *non est*, stating, "Nobody was ever home."

TRY NOT TO LET IT GET UNDER YOUR SKIN

Of course, this is still America and no amount of doorbell ringing and knocking can get someone to open their residential door when they don't want to. This is a source of great frustration among all process servers if only because it takes much more effort to serve the uncooperative subject. Yet, to many of us, the idea of employing disguises or using props such as a gift-wrapped "present" intended to deceive the subject and lure him into the open so he can be served is an idea that is unsavory, something that is amusing to hear about but not worthy of attempting. The truth is most special process servers don't go in for such ruses. We don't want to hide in trees or play dress-up. We feel it is best to be up-front and if the subject decides to avoid service at home, then we will catch him at the store or at his work where he cannot hide.

If, on your initial attempt, you suspect the subject is home but you cannot raise him, future attempts can become a sort of cat-and-mouse game. You have lost the element of surprise and this individual may be looking out for you. He may have known this lawsuit was coming, just not exactly when it was coming. The defendant sees a stranger at his door carrying a notebook that might conceal a summons, he is not going to respond. You are going to have to serve his spouse or offspring at the residence and indeed, if such relatives do exist, the defendant has instructed them to lie or otherwise obfuscate. Or, you are going to have to catch him, the defendant, out in the open. That's what I mean by a cat-and-mouse game but, emphatically, you don't want it to become a game. Games expend your energy.

It may transpire that there's nothing you can do; the defendant wants to make it a game. There is some psychology at work in which the subject sees it as a thrill or a challenge to best the pursuer, that is, the process server. I have been taunted through the front-door intercom, and I have been reported as an intruder to the police when the homeowner was fully aware of who I was and why I was there. It's the subject's way of screwing with you, and it's hard not to take it personally, but you mustn't.

Sometimes, however, taking it personally and

meeting the resistance head-on are virtually indistinguishable from one another. For example: the defendant/ respondent won't come to the door so you go to his home at 5:30 a.m. and knock, knock, knock. Somebody has to be first on your daily rounds, why not him? After two or three days of this you may wear him down; he may come out and accept service. That's not making it personal so much as it is doing what you have to do to get the job done.

Incidentally, don't be surprised if an irate/uncooperative homeowner does call the police on you for knocking at his door. This is something they never told us about in process server class. If the police do arrive, thinking to capture an intruder or lunatic, which is what the homeowner has told them, then that is actually in your favor. You have the summons and your ID card in hand to assure them that you are on the job. They've been called to answer a complaint; they want to get to the crux of the matter. Now it is John Law who is knocking on the door, looking for an explanation. Will he ignore them too? When he opens the door to speak with the police, that's your opportunity.

GAINING ACCESS

I have already addressed the notion of putting pressure on gatekeepers in the workplace who try to thwart the special process server in his mission. Any attempt to interfere with the process server who is trying to serve an employee of that establishment or the act of refusing to make that employee available for service is a misdemeanor in most states. You may have to read the law to the gatekeeper—the receptionist, the security guard, the secretary—as well as his or her boss before they see the light and decide to comply with your request.

Okay, then what about the individual who isn't being protected by a gatekeeper but is somewhat difficult to get to nonetheless?

If the subject works in a factory, for example, you want to know which shift. Sometimes human resources or personnel will tell you over the phone which shift the person works, but more often you must go to the place of employment, state your purpose and show your ID to get the information needed. With any luck, the individual will be there on your initial trip. Otherwise you will have to return during his shift.

Since time is money, being kept waiting is a real problem. I am not talking about waiting for a doctor to finish examining his patient or a psychiatrist to complete her 55-minute session; those are legitimate waits, I feel, during which time I will catch up on my reading. No, I am speaking of having to deal with the chain of command structure common to large businesses such as hospitals, factories, and corporations. Not every employee is accountable in these places and I have been kept waiting up to an hour while some supervisor on the instruction of some other supervisor half-heartedly tries to track down said employee. Meanwhile, I am wearing out my shoes pacing the lobby.

Maybe the sheriff's deputy who is salaried and earns the same whether he serves three people that day or nine, doesn't mind the wait. I resent it and so should you. If the entry is restricted, of course you will have to go through channels. But if the entry is unrestricted you might try to get to the person on your own. How do you do this? By calling ahead and finding out in which department the person works. If you know the guy works in the body shop of a car dealership, then you don't start by checking in with the business manager who then has to consult with two others before she can proceed. You go directly to the body shop to serve him forthwith, no intermediaries.

Hospitals are famous for not wanting their medical staff to be surprised or in any way put out. There is a large hospital here, in St. Louis, with protocol set up for the service of process on their employees. The procedure is to go to the security office, state your purpose, and then sit and wait and wait and wait for some guard to finally arrive at which time you will be escorted to the individual to be served. But the hospital is not on lockdown and if I can find where that individual works I will simply make a beeline to that department and ask for her. She'll probably accept the papers with a thank you. These people are not dignitaries; the process server should not have to go through so many roadblocks to get to them.

IMMUNITY FROM SERVICE

There was a time in the 19th and 20th centuries when, throughout much of the country, service of process was prohibited on a Sunday, or at least not before sundown. Such "Sabbath statutes" may still be on the books in certain states. One of them may be the state in which you work. The formalities of service, rooted in civil conduct, vary from state to state. I personally have no qualms about serving papers on Sunday, but then that is legal here in Missouri. If you are unsure about Sunday service in a certain jurisdiction, you should call the sheriff's office and inquire.

Likewise, there is a longstanding rule in civil procedure that a defendant may not be served with process at a time when, according to legal scholars Friedenthal, Kane and Miller, he has been "invited into the forum to negotiate a settlement to the dispute underlying the lawsuit. Both during travel to and from the forum for negotiations and during the stay in the forum, the defendant is immune from service of process and process served under these circumstances generally will be void."

Apparently, this ruse of flushing out an elusive defendant by falsely extending an olive branch had been employed by a plaintiff and the defendant, indignant at being tricked, challenged the service through the courts and won.

These days, the most likely forum in which a defendant would be immune from service is the courtroom. Be careful if the lawyer tells you, "Mrs. Kraus will be appearing in Division 7 on Thursday at 9 a.m. I need you to go and serve her there." You can wait for her at the entrance to the courthouse, serve her beneath the sculpture of Dame Justice if you wish. You can even serve her in the hall outside the court-room, but generally, throughout the land, you may not serve her in the court itself.

Active members of the armed forces are also gen-erally immune from service of process. Most out-of-state summons request that the server ask the defen-dant to be served whether they are currently a mem-ber of the armed forces and, if so, to withhold service.

INSURANCE

Special Process Servers are accountable for their behavior and actions and can be held to criminal liability or civil liability because of these actions. Liability insurance is primarily to protect you against lawsuits. I have already mentioned the potential for the special process server being sued by the attorney who hired him because the attorney's case was botched by improper service. Your insurance might also be seen as a buffer, some small protection against lawsuits that occur when you do something imprudent out in the field. There was recently a story in the news about a special process server in Los Angeles who was slapped with criminal charges for allegedly stalking a guy he was trying to serve. I'm not sure how that could happen—are we not required to diligently pursue ["stalk," in a manner of speaking] the defendants/respondents we are charged with serving?

At any rate, the point is you can go too far in your duties. There's a balance between an individual's right to privacy and your duty to hand him a restraining order. You can pursue the correct person too aggressively or, worse yet, the incorrect person too aggressively. Throwing stones at windows, pounding on doors, entering a dwelling without an invitation or otherwise waxing bold and reckless may not only bring on a lawsuit, it could get you shot.

While the cost of Errors and Omissions insurance is dear, currently around $550 for 12 months coverage, a special process server in demand can make this back in a week or two.

⤴

CROSSING THE LINE

As with any profession, standards of conduct are expected of members of the process-serving community. A licensed process server may lose his or her license and, as a result, the privilege to practice for failing to meet those standards. Any process server licensed by the City of St. Louis who has been accused of any number of complaints to the Circuit Court may be subject to a hearing which may result in the revocation of the special's license. The complaints include but are not limited to making a false return, impersonating a police officer or sheriff, making an unlawful entry into a residence, using excessive force, billing for work that was not performed and the unauthorized practice of law.

This last complaint is worth a discourse, because it is something any well-meaning process server could unintentionally fall into. We've all seen it happen: You hand someone a summons and the person looks at it in bewilderment. "What is this?" he asks. That's a valid question, and you can tell him it's a summons with a petition attached. "But what does it mean?" he presses. That's another valid question, but it's one you don't have to answer in any detail. You might say, "It's a lawsuit. Read it carefully and it should become clear" or "You may want to talk to a lawyer." If it's a subpoena you could say, "This is a subpoena. It commands you to be in Division 43 of the County Courts at 11 a.m. on November 4." You might point to the place on the document where the instruction is set forth.

Another question the process server often hears from the person served is the plaintive "What do I do now?" That's fishing for advice. It may be from a guy who is suddenly devastated by the thought that his children may be taken from him. You may be quite empathetic to his plight, but you must resist the temptation to "practice law," as it were, offering advice with your limited knowledge regarding just what it is that you think he must or should do. Even sticking around for a minute and listening to the defendant's diatribe against the plaintiff is a bad idea. Too much conversation with the defendant is not only unethical but illegal. Again, the safest course is to simply inform this individual what sort of legal document has been served upon him, point out the court date if applicable, and tell him that a lawyer will be able to answer additional questions.

As far as making false returns, there will be opportunity to do so. After all, it is your word, your version of what happened out there. Likely no one will come along to contest what you have stated. You may start out altering small but significant details such as the date of service. You served the defendant on the 11th of the month, a day after the summons expired. So you fudge a little and make it the 10th to keep within the allowable time frame. The kid at the door told you he was 14 and you gave him the summons and petition anyway with the instruction to pass it on to his dad. But on the affidavit you have to lie, just a little. You make him a year older because 15 is the minimum age for a family member to accept copy service. No one is going to know, right?

Or even more egregious, the defendant wasn't home so you left the process at his doorstep. You phoned his home later that day and inquired if he received his summons and petition. He affirmed so and you called it personal service on your affidavit.

Sure, you may get away with passing off these trifling little lies ninety-nine times in a row but on the hundredth time it will come back to bite you in the rump. Don't be that guy or gal, the one who violates the defendant's civil rights, just a little.

~⊕~

ADJUNCT WORK

If an attorney sees you as an asset, someone he can count on, then expect some odd jobs to come your way. Some of them are pleasant, some stressful, and some just plain bizarre. I have been hired to work as a courier, delivering legal papers to the State Supreme Court when there was no time for Federal Express. Likewise I have been a chauffeur, driving an attorney 150 miles to a county seat while he prepared his arguments sprawled out in the back seat. I have taken curbside trash, intended for the refuse truck, in order to document the contents and possibly find "dirt" on the residents.

If you are handy with a camera, you may be called to photograph accident scenes, wrecked cars in the impound lot, perilous situations, or objects in slip-and-fall cases. I once found myself in a supermarket, surreptitiously photographing negligent practices that had caused a little old lady to be run over by a produce cart, resulting in a broken pelvis and elbow.

Of course, this gets into the area of investigation, a profession in and of itself and one that can keep you as busy as you want to be. If you, the special process server, get a taste of investigation, you may come to a crossroads where you ponder whether you want to actively pursue that calling. Most process servers do a certain amount of surveillance and investigation; it comes with the territory. I like process serving and being a part of the judicial system; I try to keep the P.I. stuff to a minimum.

By the very nature of the job, however, the special process server will become adept at finding people, whether they want to be found or not. The process server as hunter/tracker is a valuable person. Sometimes the investigative side dovetails nicely with the process-serving side. For instance, a client may want to know the whereabouts of an individual whom she intends to sue. Once she knows that person is "getable," she'll file the suit. They may ask you to locate the would-be defendant and to serve the summons after you have located him.

THE PROCESS BROKERS

In every big city and certainly in every state, there are private business concerns that serve process in a wholesale fashion. Some of them deal in local paper; others work foreign paper only. They advertise in the legal periodicals; they may attend trade conventions and make important connections; they have ample resources and databases to draw from. Often, these firms have law-enforcement-sounding names such as Worldwide Investigations or Special Services and, indeed, may have ex-cops on staff. They do P.I. work, but they also take in lots of process, which they dole out to their cadre of process servers.

Some specials like working for these companies. It's steady work, true, but it is a whole different ball game from working as an independent. These broker operations will usually take one-half to two-thirds of the fee, after which, the process server who actually does the work gets the rest. If you have worked as an independent, it's hard to justify doing the same amount of work for half the fee that you would normally charge. Then again, there are times of lean when the phone is silent, no calls from attorneys to come pick up a summons. It's nice to have some work to fall back on even if the pay rates are discounted. Like lots of things in life, it's a tradeoff.

One good thing about these companies that handle volumes of process, they can give you papers that are in proximity to one another. Currently, I work for a company that provides me with some 25 papers per month, all summonses involving non-payment of child support. I could have double that number if I chose, but that is what I can handle in addition to my regular workload. These papers are sorted geographically, by zip code, so that a half-dozen visits might be limited to one confined area. What you might lose in discounted fees, you make up for in volume.

Another tradeoff involves control. Whereas the independent operates by his own set of standards and smarts, process brokers—certain ones anyway—want things done their way. There is a protocol for every aspect of the job. That's the broker's prerogative, of course, although it may be exasperating. For example, one company that I tried working for had a rule that if you didn't make service in two attempts you returned to home base, the office, for an assessment of the situation. I felt like I was perfectly capable of assessing the situation myself. They also took the summonses from me in order to run a "skip trace." I never saw those summonses again. I was kept in the dark over their disposition: *Non est?* Served? If so, by whom? Had these summonses originated from one of my lawyers, I would have been appointed by the court as special process server on the case, and I would have seen the job through from start to finish. Ultimately, I found no satisfaction working for that particular out-fit and I decided to quit. However, the work is there if you want it.

❧

LONG-DISTANCE JOBS

If you think about it, process serving is one of the most environmentally uncool occupations. Talk about generating carbon emissions, you're driving scores, even hundreds of miles just to hand someone a piece of paper. But there is something you can do to economize on travel. Say you get a summons with an address in a neighboring county and say there is plenty of time to serve this summons. You might try holding off on the initial visit for a few days to see if you will get another paper going in the same direction. If that happens, you will also get a double-dip on mileage, that is, you will be charging two separate law firms mileage for all or part of the same trip.

If you have driven 60 miles to serve a summons or subpoena and if the residents are not home, you might want to wait around. Check out the area. Find a park, read the paper, take a walk. Even if you've driven just 30 miles, you really don't want to return without result. One action, before leaving the area, might be to rap on the neighbor's doors: "I'm looking for Ralph Jackson. Do you know when he might be home?" If the neighbor asks about the nature of your business, be vague. At least don't inform them you're delivering a summons. In any event, it's possible the neighbor will turn out to be helpful, especially in small towns where distrust is not the norm. The friendly neighbor may just blurt, "Well, did you try the IGA store over on Adams? That's where he works."

Remember that in outlying areas the residence you seek may be geographically far from the town listed on the mailing address. In other words, you have a summons for Mary Farley at 3213 Bogus Lane, Imperial, Missouri 63020. You know that Imperial is in a neighboring county, so you drive the 40 miles only to learn that Bogus Lane is 15 miles outside Imperial, actually closer to the town of DeSoto, although it has an Imperial mailing address. Such an erroneous assumption costs you time and gas. If you are going to do any regular work in a county, it's wise to buy a street guide to that county. Again, MapQuest® can be very helpful, especially in the country, because the turns are expressed in distances down to the tenth of a mile and too often these country roads bear no street signs and there is nobody around to ask directions. The hardest addresses to find are those in the country.

The critical thing is to know where you are going before heading out. If the street guide or MapQuest® cannot help, you might try calling the 911 dispatcher for that county, either the sheriff department or the EMS. Explain that you are a process server and need directions to the address in question. I find that they are usually helpful in these matters.

Some specials maintain that when serving papers in another county it is a good idea to inform the sheriff of that county that you will be working in his bailiwick. This is considered professional courtesy, they say. Personally, I would do that only if I expected trouble. For instance, if I were told that the residence is a suspected meth lab or that the respondent/defendant had a history of violent behavior.

There may be times when it becomes necessary to spend a night somewhere. I once had a job to deliver seven subpoenas in two central Missouri counties, 150 miles distant from St. Louis. The witnesses were to give testimony in the trial of a man accused of stealing a tractor. Before I left, the hiring attorney went through the subpoenas one by one. "These four you have to get," he said, pointing to the documents laid on a conference table. "These others are important too, and give them your best shot but don't come back until you've served these four witnesses."

In addition to my regular fees I would bill for gas and, if need be, lodging. It was June. I had the time and the prospect of a road trip looked appealing. It was good to be a process server.

SETTING UP YOUR PRACTICE

The somewhat discouraging truth is that every lawyer who needs a special process server already has a special process server. If you intend to move in on that action you may have to wait until his process server either retires, dies, or screws up so badly that good graces are lost. But there is hope for the neophyte special process server. Each year lawyers emerge from law school afresh and are just now setting out their shingle; they will need a new cast of legal support. Also, when you do get hired on those first jobs you will serve the defendant lickety-split, turning that assignment around so quickly and with such efficacy that the hiring lawyer will not only praise your industry he or she will recommend you to their friends. There's no advertising as effective as word-of-mouth. Lastly, always have your business cards at the ready and don't forget to follow up on promising leads.

SCHEDULE AND FEES

For this special process server, the best part about the job is setting my own schedule. I am early-to-bed and early-to-rise and most mornings I am out the door around six a.m., striving to hit five or six addresses before the residents head off to work or elsewhere. I get large satisfaction knowing that I have made close to two hundred by the time the typical office worker has made his first trip to the water cooler. Of course, that's on a productive day. And some days you're hitting it, bim-bam-boom, knocking them out serially, forty bucks a shot. Other days though, it's like everyone's gone to the moon. Each door you knock on gives you the silent treatment. You would not be off-base in comparing process serving to fishing; success at both depends on a certain degree of luck.

In my practice there are six steps to run through and they are part of a perpetual cycle. The first step is to pick up the papers from the law office; the second is go out and serve the paper; the third, type up the affidavit and the invoice; the fourth is to get the affidavit of service notarized; the fifth step, which is optional, is to file the affidavit and the sheriff's return in court; and the sixth step, turn in the file-stamped affidavit and the invoice to the lawyer. Then wait to get paid.

As an independent contractor, your rates and fees are entirely up to you. Some attorneys ask for a price list of services, a menu of charges. I will freely tell anyone that I charge 40 dollars as a basic fee but that it could be more or even less, depending on the particulars. I trust that those who work with me know that I will be fair. Here are some of the factors that affect the final bill:

As of the year 2007 when gas prices are fluctuating between 2.70 and 3.15 a gallon, I charge 40 cents a mile when traveling beyond the county line. Each time I make the trip, mileage is tacked on. Sometimes the mileage will exceed the base fee. If your subject lives 60 miles away that's $48 mileage for each attempt [.40 X 120 miles round trip]. If you serve that person on the third attempt that comes to $184 or 48 +48 + 48 [mileage] +40 [basic fee]. That's the cold, hard figure before recrimination sets in. In other words, you might ask yourself: Did I make at least one of those trips at a time, say, early morning or dinner time, when I would be more likely to have success? If not, you might consider knocking a few bucks off the bill. Also, the attempts you made probably did not strictly translate to a complete round trip, that is, you didn't go from home base to the destination and return without doing any other jobs in between. You might want to shave off a few bucks more. Maybe the $184.00 bill becomes $150.00. Show your discounts on the invoice.

If you are going to be doing all this driving, you should inform the hiring attorney of the potential costs involved. He or she may tell you to forget it and get the local sheriff to do the job. Believe me, there have been many long-distance jobs that were such a hassle, that required hours and hours of drive time, that despite the fat check at the end of the job I truly wished the attorney would have trusted the local sheriff department to accomplish service.

Some process servers will use other landmarks, such as a river or an interstate highway, as a border beyond which mileage is charged. It is fair to charge mileage when traveling to the far reaches of the home county, say, 25 miles or more, although I probably would not charge for the first attempt. I'm a bit sheepish about charging mileage within the county, although it's never an issue to charge mileage for going even five miles across the Mississippi River into Illinois; after all, it's another state.

The point at which you decide to start charging mileage and the amount you decide to charge per mile are really arbitrary. Nevertheless it's a free market and, rest assured, if the hiring lawyer feels you are too steep he will find someone else to do the job.

The most difficult bill to turn in is the one where you have racked up serious mileage but failed to achieve service. In such an instance, everyone is frustrated—the lawyer, the client, and especially the process server. I once had to serve a man in Springfield, Illinois, 100 miles from home base. I made three visits, even staked out the house, and each time the trip was futile. In all, I drove 600 miles, spent three half-days in the car, and had nothing to show except a huge gas bill. Even though I had given it my best shot, I felt terrible. Still, I had to get paid for my effort and for the wear and tear on my car. I could only hope that the lawyer would not lose faith in me and decide to throw away my phone number. It is not always an attorney or law firm that hires a special to serve papers. Private individuals such as landlords or adult-abuse victims may call, having been to court and seen your name on the list. From these people you should accept advance payment. However, the work you receive from your regular lawyers should be billed after you have done the job, and that is because there are so many sudden turns involved in process serving. The jobs you imagine will be easy often turn out to be difficult, and vice-versa.

For instance, say the address on the summons turns out to be non-existent. It's not your fault; somebody made a clerical error. Still, you drove 24 miles round trip in a thunderstorm. Charge 10 or 15 dollars as a "bad-address fee." In another situation you've got a totally uncooperative subject who won't open the door and practices evasion. Yet you are instructed by the hiring lawyer that his client, the plaintiff in the lawsuit, "will pay anything to get this guy served." If you have the patience to wait outside his home to catch him at a vulnerable moment you should charge a "surveillance fee." Private investigators get $50 an hour for doing crossword puzzles in the car; charge accordingly.

Sometimes discounts are in order. For example, certain civil suits name both the husband and the wife and if they live together you can serve them simultaneously. Whichever one comes to the door will be served personally and in turn he or she will accept for the other who will thus be served by copy service. In that instance, you may consider giving a "same time, same place discount." Instead of charging $40 per person, you charge, say, $55 for both. Even though you served both summonses in one fell swoop, you must still file two notarized affidavits. That's additional paperwork.

Some specials charge a bit less for serving what is called a simple subpoena, meaning process that is directed to a business or corporation where no resistance is expected, where the server should be able to get in and out within minutes. In the structure of these businesses, there are people whose job it is to accept summonses and subpoenas; nothing could be easier for the process server. Charge what you deem fair, keeping in mind, though, that the easy jobs make up for the hard ones.

If you are in business for yourself, be prepared to have to agitate for payment. It is galling and humiliating to have to plead to be paid for work you have done but it seems it cannot be avoided. Whether it is a sizeable law firm with a business manager or a solo lawyer with only a part-time secretary, I find that my bills are too frequently lost or misplaced or end up at the bottom of the pile and stay there. The bill is turned in and a month goes by; nothing happens. You call to inquire and are told the bill is missing. Can you fax another one? Another month may go by, the same thing is repeated. It is truly a test of one's patience and forbearance. Some lawyers want to pay in advance, others pay like clockwork with a check in the mail, still others drag their feet and take a month too long, and there are even some who offer all manner of excuse and put off paying until such time as they need your services again. Which one of these lawyers are you going to go that extra mile for?

For your part, you must keep a record of each and every job you get, logging in the cases by cause number, which lawyer or law firm tendered it, date received, date due, and disposition—served or *non est*. You will notate amount paid and the date it was paid. This logbook is your bible. If you have any volume of work at all, checks will be streaming in. Your cash flow. If you forget to mark down a payment and then you start dunning the lawyer, you may just end up looking like an inept bozo.

❦

NO OTHER JOB LIKE IT

Process serving is not romantic in the Dashiell Hammett-private eye sense of the word. It is lonely work. It is grueling work, fraught with disappointment and stress. Imagine driving 70 miles into the pre-dawn countryside only to find that your target has left five minutes before you arrived. Imagine knocking long on the door of a residence with shades and blinds shut tight as a tomb and yet you can hear people within. Imagine knocking on the door of a residence and the only sign of life is a face that appears in an upper-floor window, merely staring down at you. Imagine being screamed at, being mocked, being lied to over and over. It is a righteous test of one's mettle. Yet, if you are tenacious all the adverse circumstances, all the bad luck in the world may not be able to bridle you. You may well prevail— and that is one of the finest feelings in the world, achieving service against the odds.

And there are few jobs that offer such insight to the human condition. You see people at their worst, when they are thrust into a tantrum over having received a lawsuit. You see people at their best when they graciously accept service without a fuss. The special process server—summoner, courier, sleuth—sees it all.

LEXICON

Some common legal terms used in
process serving and on court papers:

alias: As in "alias summons." The service has been
attempted once before

defendant / respondent: The person who is the target
of the lawsuit

et al: Latin for "and others"

et ux: Latin for "and wife"

et curia: Latin for "out of court"

ex parte: Latin for "out of the hearing of"; a one-
sided hearing. A judge issues an ex parte order of protection based on the petitioner's story and plea for help

ex rel: Latin for "on the relation"; a proceeding instituted by the Attorney General in name and on behalf of the State but at the instigation of the individual

non est: Latin for "did not happen"; unable to serve the process

plaintiff / petitioner: The person bringing the lawsuit

petition or complaint: A document crafted by a lawyer which is attached to the summons stating the facts of the lawsuit and setting forth the sum demanded for damages

pluries: As in "pluries summons." The service has been attempted at least twice before

process: A legal document to be served upon an individual or business entity; sometimes called "papers"

subpoena: From the Latin, literally "under punishment." A paper served to compel an individual to appear and give testimony [*subpoena ad testificandum*] or to appear and produce documents [*subpoena duces tecum*]

summons: A document issued by the office of the circuit clerk and attached to the petition. The summons contains the style of the case and other pertinent information to be read by the defendant once he or she is served

AFTERWORD
❧ ❧ ❧

Readers of this excellent handbook will no doubt come away from this text with two lessons learned. First, the system does not work unless the summons or subpoena gets served. Second, when you do serve the papers, do it right.

As a judge in predominantly "high volume" divisions, I see every day the effect, or lack of effect, the service of process has on the system. A lawyer who is unable to obtain service on his opponent or crucial witness has no case. When there is no case, the case is dismissed for lack of attention. People are well-skilled in avoiding the process or system. The sheriff trying to serve the evader has 50 other documents to serve and so will only devote as much time as he can, which is not much at all. This is where the "special" comes in. Without a diligent special working the case, the case may die—commerce halts and the world as we know it ends. This last statement may be melodramatic, but it is said for the purpose of highlighting the importance of the non-sheriff process server.

Now, having gained service, the next question for the system is: Was the service good? This handbook offers sound technical rules for proper service. I have seen from the bench many a case dissolve because the special served the wrong person, served a person of the household who was too young or just plain did not serve anyone but claimed in the affidavit that he or she had. There are many reasons why a judge may set aside a judgment, and too often some of them can be laid at the foot of the careless process server.

This book not only provides the technical rules for proper service but describes what I think is the proper temperament or demeanor a process server should have. These traits include taking one's time and getting to know the target by asking questions and getting a description.

I can think of few jobs more stressful than process serving. You see people at their worst at a time when they receive the very unpleasant news that they are now a party in a lawsuit or being called as a witness to a trial or hearing. This book is an excellent guide in accomplishing the goal of service as well as how to do it right the first time.

So, if you're interested in becoming a special, first learn the rules and follow them judiciously. And remember, be careful out there.

Judge John F. Garvey
22nd Judicial Circuit
St. Louis, Missouri

OTHER BOOKS BY WM. STAGE
ↁ ↁ ↁ

Ghost Signs: Brick Wall Signs In America, 1989

Mound City Chronicles, 1991

Litchfield: A Strange And Twisted Saga Of Murder In The Midwest, 1998

Have A Weird Day: Reflections And Ruminations On The St. Louis Experience, 2003

Pictures Of People, 2005

Do The Wrong Thing, 2007

Since 1982, Wm. Stage has been a feature writer and columnist for several periodicals including the *Christian Science Monitor*, the *St. Louis Post-Dispatch* and the *St. Charles County* [Missouri] *Business Record*. In 1998, he became a special process server and since has tried to balance the two careers of journalism and legal services. Stage holds a Bachelor of Philosophy degree [BPh.] from Thomas Jefferson College, Grand Valley State University, Allendale, Michigan. He also served in the U.S. Army Medical Corps during the Vietnam conflict [1969-1972] as well as in the Air Force Reserves [1983-1991]. A lover of taverns and alleyways, he lives with his dog, Jack, on The Hill neighborhood of St. Louis.

ACKNOWLEDGMENTS

Special thanks to those who helped including the Hon. Jimmie M. Edwards, Circuit Judge 22nd Judicial Circuit of Missouri; Major Greg Thomas, Sheriff Department, City of St. Louis; and Mary Gardner, proof reader.

Birkenfeld Press is an imprint
of Floppinfish Publishing Co. Ltd.
Post Office Box 4932
St. Louis, Missouri 63108
314.567.8697

floppinfish
publishing co. ltd.